Meet Ba...

H... ...chet a... ...n, an... ... ...s Barbara Shaffer. The California crochet designer inherited her fondness for the craft from her great-grandmother.

We asked Barbara how she develops her designs. "I don't plan a design," she says. "It just comes to me. Sometimes I see a pattern in my sleep. The work is always trial-and-error until I'm holding what I've envisioned."

Barbara's four children are grown now, which gives her more time for designing. Her other interests include organic cooking and gardening. To find more publications filled with Barbara's innovative crochet projects, visit **LeisureArts.com**.

Fun to Wear Tube Scarves

...carves may be the most useful, stylish accessories you can crochet in just a short time—
...d wearing these tube scarves is just plain fun! The five designs offer fascinating pattern ...itches, as well as original finishing treatments for the ends of each scarf. Choose your ...vorite yarns and spice up your wardrobe with creative, colorful tube scarves!

What's Inside

Leisure Arts, Inc.
Little Rock Arkansas

Blushing Beauty

■■■□ INTERMEDIATE

Finished Size: 3½" x 85"
(9 cm x 216 cm)

MATERIALS

LIGHT 3

Light Weight Yarn
[3 ounces, 237 yards
85 grams, 217 meters) per
skein]: 3 skeins
Crochet hook, size J (6 mm)
or size needed for gauge

GAUGE: In pattern,
27 sts = 3½" (9 cm) and
8 rnds = 4¼" (10.75 cm)

Gauge Swatch: 3½" w x 4¼" h
(9 cm x 10.75 cm)
Work same as Scarf for
8 rnds.

BACK POST DOUBLE CROCHET

(abbreviated BPdc)
YO, insert hook from **back**
to **front** around post of st
indicated *(Fig. 1, page 32)*,
YO and pull up a loop
(3 loops on hook), (YO and
draw through 2 loops on
hook) twice.

FRONT POST DOUBLE CROCHET

(abbreviated FPdc)
YO, insert hook from **front**
to **back** around post of st
indicated *(Fig. 1, page 32)*,
YO and pull up a loop
(3 loops on hook), (YO and
draw through 2 loops on
hook) twice.

FRONT POST TREBLE CROCHET
(abbreviated FPtr)
YO twice, insert hook from **front** to **back** around post of st indicated *(Fig. 1, page 32)*, YO and pull up a loop (4 loops on hook), (YO and draw through 2 loops on hook) 3 times.

BEGINNING POPCORN
(uses one st or sp)
Ch 3, 3 dc in same st or sp, drop loop from hook, insert hook from **front** to **back** in first dc of 4-dc group, hook dropped loop and draw through st, ch 1 to close.

POPCORN
(uses one st or sp)
4 Dc in st or sp indicated, drop loop from hook, insert hook from **front** to **back** in first dc of 4-dc group, hook dropped loop and draw through st, ch 1 to close.

SCARF
Ch 27; being careful not to twist ch, join with slip st to form a ring.

Rnd 1 (Right side): Ch 3 **(counts as first dc, now and throughout)**, dc in next ch and in each ch around; join with slip st to first dc: 27 dc.

Note: Loop a short piece of yarn around any stitch to mark Rnd 1 as **right** side.

Rnd 2: Ch 1, work BPdc around same st and around each of next 4 dc, skip next dc, work FPdc around each of next 3 dc, working in **front** of last 3 FPdc made, FPtr around skipped dc, ★ work BPdc around each of next 5 dc, skip next dc, work FPdc around each of next 3 dc, working in **front** of last 3 FPdc made, FPtr around skipped dc; repeat from ★ around; join with slip st to first BPdc.

Rnd 3: Ch 1, work BPdc around same st and around each of next 4 sts, work FPdc around each of next 4 sts, ★ work BPdc around each of next 5 sts, work FPdc around each of next 4 sts; repeat from ★ around; join with slip st to first BPdc.

Rnds 4 and 5: Ch 3, dc in next 4 sts, work FPdc around each of next 4 sts, ★ dc in next 5 sts, work FPdc around each of next 4 sts; repeat from ★ around; join with slip st to first dc.

Rnd 6: Ch 1, work BPdc around same st and around each of next 4 dc, skip next st, work FPdc around each of next 3 sts, working in **front** of last 3 FPdc made, FPtr around skipped dc, ★ work BPdc around each of next 5 dc, skip next st, work FPdc around each of next 3 sts, working in **front** of last 3 FPdc made, FPtr around skipped st; repeat from ★ around; join with slip st to first BPdc.

Repeat Rnds 3-6 for pattern until Scarf measures approximately 80" (203 cm) from beginning ch, ending by working Rnd 3, do **not** finish off.

EDGING
FIRST END
Rnd 1: Work beginning Popcorn, ★ ch 1, skip next st, work Popcorn in next st; repeat from ★ around to last 2 sts, ch 1, skip last 2 sts; join with slip st to top of beginning Popcorn: 13 Popcorns.

Rnds 2 and 3: Slip st in next ch-1 sp, work beginning Popcorn in same sp, ch 1, ★ work Popcorn in next ch-1 sp, ch 1; repeat from ★ around; join with slip st to top of beginning Popcorn.

Rnd 4: Slip st in next ch-1 sp, ch 1, sc in same sp, ch 4, sc in third ch from hook, ch 1, ★ sc in next ch-1 sp, ch 4, sc in third ch from hook, ch 1; repeat from ★ around; join with slip st to first sc, finish off.

SECOND END

Rnd 1: With **right** side facing and working in free loops of beginning ch *(Fig. 2, page 32)*, join yarn with slip st in any ch; work beginning Popcorn, ★ ch 1, skip next ch, work Popcorn in next ch; repeat from ★ around to last 2 chs, ch 1, skip last 2 chs; join with slip st to top of beginning Popcorn: 13 Popcorns.

Complete same as First End, beginning with Rnd 2.

Pastel Pleaser

■■■□ INTERMEDIATE

Finished Size: 4½" x 52"
(11.5 cm x 132 cm)

MATERIALS
Light Weight Yarn
[2.4 ounces, 185 yards
(70 grams, 169 meters) per
skein**]**: 4 skeins
Crochet hook, size G (4 mm)
or size needed for gauge

GAUGE: In pattern,
48 sts = 4½" (11.5 cm)
and 11 rnds = 4" (10 cm)

Gauge Swatch: 4½" w x 4" h
(11.5 cm x 10 cm)
Work same as Scarf for
11 rnds.

STITCH GUIDE
BACK POST DOUBLE CROCHET
(abbreviated BPdc)
YO, insert hook from **back**
to **front** around post of st
indicated *(Fig. 1, page 32)*,
YO and pull up a loop
(3 loops on hook), (YO and
draw through 2 loops on
hook) twice.

LIGHT 3

SCARF

Ch 48; being careful not to twist ch, join with slip st to form a ring.

Rnd 1 (Right side): Ch 3 **(counts as first dc, now and throughout)**, dc in next ch and in each ch around; join with slip st to first dc: 48 dc.

Note: Loop a short piece of yarn around any stitch to mark Rnd 1 as **right** side.

Rnd 2: Ch 1, work BPdc around same st and around each st around; join with slip st to first BPdc.

Rnd 3: Ch 6 **(counts as first dc plus ch 3)**, dc in same st, skip next 3 sts, ★ (dc, ch 3, dc) in next st, skip next 3 sts; repeat from ★ around; join with slip st to first dc: 12 ch-3 sps and 24 dc.

Rnd 4: Ch 3, 2 dc in next ch-3 sp, ★ dc in next 2 dc, 2 dc in next ch-3 sp; repeat from ★ around to last dc, dc in last dc; join with slip st to first dc.

Repeat Rnds 2-4 for pattern until Scarf measures approximately 52" (132 cm) from beginning ch, ending by working Rnd 2; finish off.

Cloud White

Finished Size: 4" x 85"
(10 cm x 216 cm)

MATERIALS
Light Weight Yarn [LIGHT 3]
[3 ounces, 237 yards
(85 grams, 217 meters) per
skein]: 3 skeins
Crochet hook, size J (6 mm)
or size needed for gauge

GAUGE: In pattern,
32 sts = 4" (10 cm) and
8 rnds = 4¼" (10.75 cm)

Gauge Swatch: 4" w x 4¼" h
(10 cm x 10.75 cm)
Work same as Scarf for
8 rnds.

STITCH GUIDE
FRONT POST DOUBLE CROCHET

(abbreviated FPdc)

YO, insert hook from **front** to **back** around post of st indicated *(Fig. 1, page 32)*, YO and pull up a loop (3 loops on hook), (YO and draw through 2 loops on hook) twice.

BACK POST DOUBLE CROCHET

(abbreviated BPdc)

YO, insert hook from **back** to **front** around post of st indicated *(Fig. 1, page 32)*, YO and pull up a loop (3 loops on hook), (YO and draw through 2 loops on hook) twice.

SCARF

Ch 32; being careful not to twist ch, join with slip st to form a ring.

Rnd 1 (Right side)**:** Ch 1, (sc, ch 2, 3 dc) in same ch, skip next 3 chs, ★ (sc, ch 2, 3 dc) in next ch, skip next 3 chs; repeat from ★ around; join with slip st to first sc: 8 sc, 8 ch-2 sps, and 24 dc.

Note: Loop a short piece of yarn around any stitch to mark Rnd 1 as **right** side.

Rnd 2: Slip st in next ch-2 sp, ch-1, sc in same sp, ch 3, skip next 3 dc, ★ sc in next ch-2 sp, ch 3, skip next 3 dc; repeat from ★ around; join with slip st to first sc: 8 sc and 8 ch-3 sps.

Rnd 3: Ch 3 (**counts as first dc**), dc in next ch and in each ch and sc around; join with slip st to first dc: 32 dc.

Rnd 4: Ch 1, work FPdc around same st and around next dc, work BPdc around next 2 dc, ★ work FPdc around next 2 dc, work BPdc around next 2 dc; repeat from ★ around; join with slip st to first FPdc: 16 FPdc and 16 BPdc.

Rnds 5 and 6: Ch 1, work FPdc around same st and around next st, work BPdc around next 2 sts, ★ work FPdc around next 2 sts, work BPdc around next 2 sts; repeat from ★ around; join with slip st to first FPdc: 16 FPdc and 16 BPdc.

Rnd 7: Ch 1, (sc, ch 2, 3 dc) in same st, skip next 3 sts, ★ (sc, ch 2, 3 dc) in next st, skip next 3 sts; repeat from around; join with slip st to first sc: 8 sc, 8 ch-2 sps, and 24 dc.

Repeat Rnds 2-7 for pattern until piece measures approximately 85" (216 cm) from beginning ch, ending by working Rnd 7; finish off.

Tie a knot in each end.

Wrapsody in Blue

Finished Size: 5" x 73"
(12.75 cm x 185.5 cm)

MATERIALS

Light Weight Yarn ![LIGHT 3]
[3 ounces, 237 yards
(85 grams, 217 meters) per
skein**]**: 3 skeins
Crochet hook, size J (6 mm)
or size needed for gauge

GAUGE: In pattern,
36 sts = 5" (12.75 cm) and
7 rnds = 3¼" (8.25 cm)

Gauge Swatch: 5" w x 3¼" h
(12.75 cm x 8.25 cm)
Ch 36; being careful not to
twist ch, join with slip st to
form a ring.
Rnd 1: Ch 3 **(counts as first
dc)**, dc in next ch and in each
ch around; join with slip st to
first dc: 36 dc.
Rnds 2-7: Work Rnds 12-17
of Scarf.
Finish off.

19

STITCH GUIDE
FRONT POST DOUBLE CROCHET

(abbreviated FPdc)
YO, insert hook from **front** to **back** around post of st indicated *(Fig. 1, page 32)*, YO and pull up a loop (3 loops on hook), (YO and draw through 2 loops on hook) twice.

BACK POST DOUBLE CROCHET

(abbreviated BPdc)
YO, insert hook from **back** to **front** around post of st indicated *(Fig. 1, page 32)*, YO and pull up a loop (3 loops on hook), (YO and draw through 2 loops on hook) twice.

SCARF

Ch 36; being careful not to twist ch, join with slip st to form a ring.

Rnd 1 (Right side)**:** Ch 4 **(counts as first dc plus ch 1, now and throughout)**, skip next ch, ★ dc in next ch, ch 1, skip next ch; repeat from ★ around; join with slip st to first dc: 18 dc and 18 ch-1 sps.

Note: Loop a short piece of yarn around any stitch to mark Rnd 1 as **right** side.

Rnds 2-10: Ch 4, skip next ch-1 sp, ★ dc in next dc, ch 1, skip next ch-1 sp; repeat from ★ around; join with slip st to first dc.

Rnd 11: Ch 3 (**counts as first dc**), dc in next ch-1 sp and in each dc and ch-1 sp around; join with slip st to first dc: 36 dc.

Rnd 12: Ch 1, work FPdc around same st, work BPdc around each of next 5 sts, ★ work FPdc around next st, work BPdc around each of next 5 sts; repeat from ★ around; join with slip st to first FPdc: 6 FPdc and 30 BPdc.

Rnd 13: Ch 1, work FPdc around same st and around next st, work BPdc around each of next 3 sts, ★ work FPdc around each of next 3 sts, work BPdc around each of next 3 sts; repeat from ★ around to last st, work FPdc around last st; join with slip st to first FPdc: 18 FPdc and 18 BPdc.

Rnd 14: Ch 1, work FPdc around same st and around each of next 2 sts, work BPdc around next st, ★ work FPdc around each of next 5 sts, work BPdc around next st; repeat from ★ around to last 2 sts, work FPdc around each of last 2 sts; join with slip st to first FPdc: 6 BPdc and 30 FPdc.

Rnd 15: Repeat Rnd 13.

Rnd 16: Repeat Rnd 12.

Rnd 17: Ch 4, skip next st,
★ dc in next st, ch 1, skip
next st; repeat from ★ around;
join with slip st to first dc.

Repeat Rnds 11-17 for
pattern until piece measures
approximately 66" (167.5 cm)
from beginning ch, ending by
working Rnd 16.

Last 10 Rnds: Repeat Rnd 17,
10 times.

Finish off.

Rose Garden

Finished Size: 4" x 56"
(10 cm x 142 cm)

MATERIALS
Light Weight Yarn
LIGHT 3
[3 ounces, 237 yards
(85 grams, 217 meters) per
skein]: 2 skeins
Crochet hook, size I (5.5 mm)
or size needed for gauge

GAUGE: In pattern,
50 sts = 4" (10 cm) and
7 rnds = x 4¼" (10.75 cm)

Gauge Swatch: 4" w x 4¼" h
(10 cm x 10.75 cm)
Work same as Scarf for
7 rnds.

STITCH GUIDE

SHELL (uses one st or sp) (2 dc, ch 1, 2 dc) in st or sp indicated.

FRONT POST TREBLE CROCHET

(abbreviated FPtr)
YO twice, insert hook from **front** to **back** around post of st indicated *(Fig. 1, page 32)*, YO and pull up a loop (4 loops on hook), (YO and draw through 2 loops on hook) 3 times.

SCARF

Ch 50; being careful not to twist ch, join with slip st to form a ring.

Rnd 1 (Right side)**:** Ch 3 **(counts as first dc, now and throughout)**, (dc, ch 1, 2 dc) in same ch, skip next 4 chs, ★ work Shell in next ch, skip next 4 chs; repeat from ★ around; join with slip st to first dc: 40 dc and 10 ch-1 sps.

Note: Loop a short piece of yarn around any stitch to mark Rnd 1 as **right** side.

Rnd 2: Ch 2, work FPtr around same dc, ch 3, ★ skip next 2 dc, work FPtr around each of next 2 dc (last dc of same Shell and first dc of next Shell), ch 3; repeat from ★ around to last 3 dc, skip next 2 dc, work FPtr around last dc; join with slip st to first FPtr: 10 ch-3 sps and 20 FPtr.

Rnd 3: Slip st in next ch-3 sp, ch 3, (dc, ch 1, 2 dc) in same sp, work Shell in next ch-3 sp and in each ch-3 sp around; join with slip st to first dc: 40 dc and 10 ch-1 sps.

Rnds 4-10: Repeat Rnds 2 and 3, 3 times; then repeat Rnd 2 once **more**.

Rnd 11: Ch 1, 5 sc in each ch-3 sp around; join with slip st to first sc: 50 sc.

Rnds 12 and 13: Skip next 2 sc, 5 sc in next sc, ★ skip next 4 sc, 5 sc in next sc; repeat from ★ around to last 2 sc, skip last 2 sc; join with slip st to first sc.

Rnd 14: Skip next 2 sc, slip st in next sc, ch 3, (dc, ch 1, 2 dc) in same st, ★ skip next 4 sc, work Shell in next sc; repeat from ★ around to last 2 sc, skip last 2 sc; join with slip st to first dc.

Rnds 15-23: Repeat Rnds 2 and 3, 4 times; then repeat Rnd 2 once **more**.

Repeat Rnds 11-23 for pattern until Scarf measures approximately 56" (142 cm) from beginning ch, ending by working Rnd 23.

Finish off.

TIES (Make 2)

Ch 70, sc in second ch from hook and in each ch across; finish off.

Weave one Tie through sps at each end of Scarf, and tie in a bow.

General Instructions

ABBREVIATIONS

BPdc	Back Post double crochet(s)
ch(s)	chain(s)
cm	centimeters
dc	double crochet(s)
FPdc	Front Post double crochet(s)
FPtr	Front Post treble crochet(s)
mm	millimeters
Rnd(s)	Round(s)
sc	single crochet(s)
sp(s)	space(s)
st(s)	stitch(es)
YO	yarn over

★ — work instructions following ★ as many **more** times as indicated in addition to the first time.

( ) or [ ] — work enclosed instructions **as many** times as specified by the number immediately following **or** work all enclosed instructions in the stitch or space indicated **or** contains explanatory remarks.

colon (:) — the numbers given after a colon at the end of a round denote the number of stitches you should have on that round.

●□□□ BEGINNER	Projects for first-time crocheters using basic stitches. Minimal shaping.
●●□□ EASY	Projects using yarn with basic stitches, repetitive stitch patterns, simple color changes, and simple shaping and finishing.
●●●□ INTERMEDIATE	Projects using a variety of techniques, such as basic lace patterns or color patterns, mid-level shaping and finishing.
●●●● EXPERIENCED	Projects with intricate stitch patterns, techniques and dimension, such as non-repeating patterns, multi-color techniques, fine threads, small hooks, detailed shaping and refined finishing.

CROCHET TERMINOLOGY		
UNITED STATES		INTERNATIONAL
slip stitch (slip st)	=	single crochet (sc)
single crochet (sc)	=	double crochet (dc)
half double crochet (hdc)	=	half treble crochet (htr)
double crochet (dc)	=	treble crochet(tr)
treble crochet (tr)	=	double treble crochet (dtr)
double treble crochet (dtr)	=	triple treble crochet (ttr)
triple treble crochet (tr tr)	=	quadruple treble crochet (qtr)
skip	=	miss

CROCHET HOOKS													
U.S.	B-1	C-2	D-3	E-4	F-5	G-6	H-8	I-9	J-10	K-10½	N	P	Q
Metric - mm	2.25	2.75	3.25	3.5	3.75	4	5	5.5	6	6.5	9	10	15

GAUGE

Exact gauge is **essential** for proper size. Before beginning your project, make the sample swatch given in the individual instructions in the yarn and hook specified. After completing the swatch, measure it, counting your stitches and rounds carefully. If your swatch is larger or smaller than specified, **make another, changing hook size to get the correct gauge.** Keep trying until you find the size hook that will give you the specified gauge. Once proper gauge is obtained, measure width of piece approximately every 3" (7.5 cm) to be sure gauge remains consistent.

HINTS

As in all crocheted pieces, good finishing techniques make a big difference in the quality of the piece. Make a habit of taking care of loose ends as you work. Thread a yarn needle with the yarn end. With **wrong** side facing, weave the needle through several stitches, then reverse the direction and weave it back through several stitches. When ends are secure, clip them off close to work.

Yarn Weight Symbol & Names	LACE 0	SUPER FINE 1	FINE 2	LIGHT 3	MEDIUM 4	BULKY 5	SUPER BULKY 6
Type of Yarns in Category	Fingering, 10-count crochet thread	Sock, Fingering Baby	Sport, Baby	DK, Light Worsted	Worsted, Afghan, Aran	Chunky, Craft, Rug	Bulky, Roving
Crochet Gauge* Ranges in Single Crochet to 4" (10 cm)	32-42 double crochets**	21-32 sts	16-20 sts	12-17 sts	11-14 sts	8-11 sts	5-9 sts
Advised Hook Size Range	Steel*** 6,7,8 Regular hook B-1	B-1 to E-4	E-4 to 7	7 to I-9	I-9 to K-10.5	K-10.5 to M-13	M-13 and larger

*GUIDELINES ONLY: The chart above reflects the most commonly used gauges and hook sizes for specific yarn categories.

** Lace weight yarns are usually crocheted on larger-size hooks to create lacy openwork patterns. Accordingly, a gauge range is difficult to determine. Always follow the gauge stated in your pattern.

*** Steel crochet hooks are sized differently from regular hooks–the higher the number the smaller the hook, which is the reverse of regular hook sizing.

POST STITCH

Work around post of stitch indicated, inserting hook in direction of arrow *(Fig. 1)*.

Fig. 1

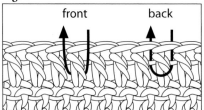

FREE LOOPS OF A CHAIN

When instructed to work in free loops of a chain, work in loop indicated by arrow *(Fig. 2)*.

Fig. 2

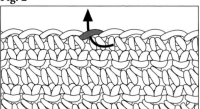

Yarn Information

The scarves in this leaflet were made using light weight yarn. Any brand of light weight yarn may be used. It is best to refer to the yardage/meters when determining how many balls or skeins to purchase. Remember, to achieve the same look, it is the weight of yarn that is important, not the brand of yarn.

We have made every effort to ensure that these instructions are accurate and complete. We cannot, however, be responsible for human error, typographical mistakes, or variations in individual work.

Production Team: Technical Writer/Editor – Joan Beebe, Jean Guirguis, Peggy Greig; Editorial Writer - Susan McManus Johnson; Senior Graphic Artist - Lora Puls; Graphic Artist - Jane Fay; Photography Manager - Katherine Laughlin; Photo Stylist - Cora Holdaway; and Photographer - Jason Masters

For digital downloads of Leisure Arts' best-selling designs, visit http://www.leisureartslibrary.com